WITHDRAWN

A Guy's Guide to Cooking

KICK-ASS

Food

DUDEFOOD

dan churchill

SIMON & SCHUSTER PAPERBACKS

New York · London · Toronto · Sydney · New Delhi

Simon & Schuster Paperbacks
An Imprint of Simon & Schuster, Inc.
1230 Avenue of the Americas
New York, NY 10020

First Simon & Schuster trade paperback edition April 2015

SIMON & SCHUSTER PAPERBACKS and colophon are registered trademarks of Simon & Schuster, Inc.

For information about special discounts for bulk purchases, please contact Simon & Schuster Special Sales at 1-866-506-1949 or business@simonandschuster.com.

The Simon & Schuster Speakers Bureau can bring authors to your live event. For more information or to book an event contact the Simon & Schuster Speakers Bureau at 1-866-248-3049 or visit our website at www.simonspeakers.com.

Interior design by Joy O'Meara

Manufactured in the United States of America

10   9   8   7   6   5   4   3   2   1

Library of Congress Cataloging-in-Publication Data
Churchill, Dan.
  Dudefood : a guy's guide to cooking kick-ass food / Dan Churchill.
     pages cm
  1. Cooking. 2. Male cooks. I. Title.
  TX714.C4963 2015
  641.5—dc23

                    2014036527

ISBN 978-1-4767-9689-5
ISBN 978-1-4767-9690-1 (ebook)

PHOTO CREDITS

I'd like to thank Karen Watson, Michael Marchment, and Isabelle Selby for their amazing work. This book would not look the same without your photographs. You're all true legends.

Karen Watson/Karen Watson Photography: ii, x, xii, 2, 3, 4, 7, 8, 10,12,15,16,18, 20, 22, 25, 26, 28, 31, 34, 36, 38, 40, 42, 44, 46, 48, 50, 52, 54, 56, 59, 64, 66, 70, 72, 74, 76, 78, 82, 87, 88, 90, 92, 94, 96, 98, 100, 102, 104, 107, 108, 110, 112, 116, 120,122, 124

Michael Marchment/The Mil Studios: 32, 68, 80, 84, 114, 118

Isabelle Selby/Isabelle Selby Photography: 144

I am the person I am today because of you.
It was through your support, constructive feedback,
sacrifices, and love that I was able to begin my journey.
You have taught me to not let anyone stand in the way
of my dreams, no matter how high I aim.

**For the things you have done,
are doing, and will do,
I dedicate this book to you,
Mum, Dad, Brendan, and Andrew.**

CONTENTS

FINGER-LICKING FEEDS

SUPER SIDES

HOW TO IMPRESS A GIRL

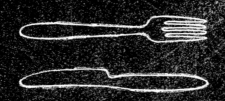

I was just starting out as a personal trainer and hadn't even attended a weekend cooking class when I wrote the first drafts of the recipes in this book. But I had always loved to eat, and I had been cooking since I was twelve years old. I remember picking fresh lemons from the backyard, using them in a curd, and turning them into Dad's lemon meringue pie. I loved creating my own hamburger patties with fresh herbs and homemade tomato sauce for Friday-night football with my mates. I developed a habit of making fresh pasta and perfected an Italian favorite of my own. It's probably one of the most cherished moments I share with my mum, dad, and two brothers. And when I wanted to impress a girl, I had that special recipe for her, too: shortbread layered with chocolate ganache and raspberries.

My mates began realizing how much their girlfriends and mums loved the fact that I could cook. They asked for my help. Over time, as I wrote and revised recipes to share with my friends, I started to realize I was writing a cookbook. So while I did not have professional experience in some of the world's best-known restaurants, I had firsthand experience cooking simple, healthy, delicious, and fun meals for the people I loved. I wanted to teach other young men to do the same.

Drawing on my time in the kitchen and the knowledge I gained from my postgraduate degree in exercise science, I wrote *DudeFood*. Not sure what to cook when trying to impress a girl? Undecided on what to create at your next barbecue with your mates? Wondering what would make the

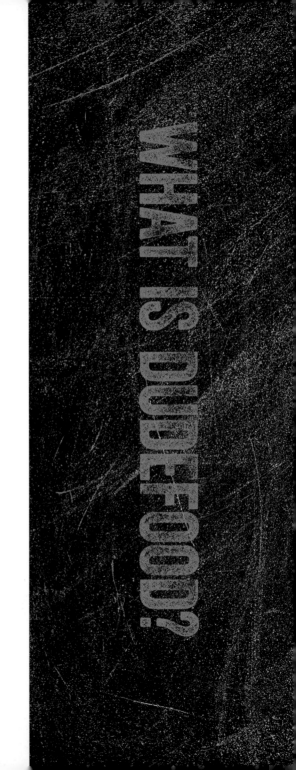

WHAT IS DUDEFOOD?

perfect post-workout meal? I have been in your shoes. *DudeFood* is organized to provide an easy-to-understand method to decide what to cook in particular situations.

Throughout this book, I have incorporated handy hints to help you develop your skills in the kitchen. A pantry stocked with simple ingredients holds endless possibilities. You don't always have to stick to the recipes—alter the ingredients to your taste. (Although, while you may like garlic, if you're cooking for a date, go easy.) I've also noted places where you can make a few substitutions if you'd like to make a classic dish better for your waistline.

Get involved. Don't be afraid to make mistakes. If you burn your potatoes, you've learned to lower the heat next time. If the center of your fish is underdone, you've learned to keep it in the pan for a few more minutes. We all start somewhere. All of this takes a bit of practice, but *DudeFood* can be

your guide. It can show you how to be the master of your own kitchen.

You won't need a food dictionary to follow along. All of the ingredients listed here can be found in your local grocery store. I promised my mates I would not include anything in my recipes that they have never heard of, let alone spelled. I wrote *DudeFood* in a language I like to call "colloquial dude." Cheers, brah!

I'm happy to share the secrets that will make your new life of cooking simple, healthy, delicious, and fun. Go ask five lovely ladies if they like a man who can cook. Now, I am not a betting man, but I am very confident about the smiles and winks you will receive from their end.

DudeFood will unlock a potential most young men never thought they had. Trust me: You can turn your bowl of cereal into a breakfast spread fit for a king, or in your case, a Dude.

The Problem

DudeFood was created to educate, motivate, and inspire an intimidated male audience. A recent study found that 90 percent of women in Australia were not happy with the quality of men in Australia. Among those interviewed, their number one concern was cooking. Gone are the days of the stereotypical housewife, when the men earned the bread and the women would slave away cooking—but although the times have changed, many men seem to have maintained this mentality.

I've also noticed that more and more people around my age stay at their parents' house after graduation, where the cleaning, washing, and cooking are taken care of (rather than learning these skills themselves).

Whether it is a challenge or an unforeseen expectation, men find it hard to motivate themselves to get behind a stove or put on those oven mitts. There are exceptions, of course, as a lot of men enjoy the art of mixing quality produce with a wooden spoon, but I've noticed that many of my mates tend to avoid the kitchen.

The Solution

It's not that guys don't want to cook—they're often intimidated by long ingredient lists and pages of directions. Remember that first time riding a bike? Things take practice. My hope is that this book will act like training wheels. *DudeFood* is the first step. Turn on that stove: You'll be surprised how easy cooking will be.

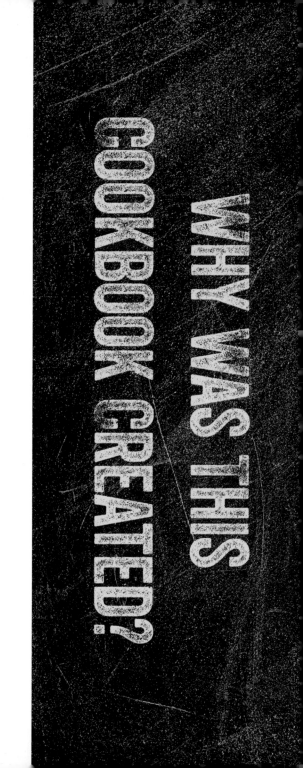

WHY WAS THIS COOKBOOK CREATED?

The Health Benefit

We have been taught to do things the easy way, regardless of the impact it will have on our health. Ordering takeout harms more than our wallets. Lack of knowledge is a major part of the problem. Not many teenagers were involved enough with meal planning at home, and when they decided to leave, they were not prepared for the demands of making a quality, healthy meal.

If a microwave is your best friend, you need to learn how to turn your oven on. If you are calling in orders to Chinese takeout restaurants three times a week, you need to learn what a skillet can do. Start off simple and cook a rump steak or even just an egg with some steamed vegetables. This may be a plain, basic meal but it contains more nutri-ents than you have been having for the past two weeks.

The Romantic Perk

Men do not realize the appeal cooking has to their partner. If you have not taken the hint, when the meat is left out defrosting with your name on it, then this will let you know: Women love a man who can cook. One, it shows a man can look after himself, and two, what is sexier than seeing a man in nothing but an apron? So prepare a dinner for two. Here is a tip: Choose a red meat to go with a red wine. This will increase serotonin (sex hormone) levels and be sure to result in a trip to the bedroom.

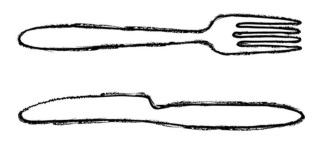

How often have you come home and wanted a marinated steak? There is nothing more satisfying than sitting down with a full meal in front you, cooked just the way you want it. The ability to cook is an important life skill. Relying on someone else to provide you with the necessary nutrients demonstrates a lack of independence.

And if you haven't taken the hint, girls love a guy who can speak through food. Do you want that extra appeal? Get behind the barbecue, put that apron on, and show off your knife skills.

Food is a great way to bring people together. How many guys have been starving on a Saturday at lunchtime and gone down to the local burger shop and picked up a battered chicken burger with a measly bit of lettuce saturated in mayonnaise? Sounds satisfying. . . . Instead, why not get the boys together and make your own marinated grilled chicken on a bun you know is not comprised of sugar? It doesn't have to be swimming in mayonnaise and you can add whatever components you want. Best of all, you have found an awesome way to get the boys together for a beer.

When the word *cooking* comes to mind, what are your thoughts? Hard, time-consuming, cleaning? I'll be honest in saying that I hate cleaning up; however, I have learned how to, as girls call it, "clean as you go." As for it being hard and time-consuming, well, practice makes perfect, and you can make whatever you want—so it doesn't have to be hard. If you make a mistake, you may have invented a new pasta sauce. It all starts from your original frame of mind. Before

you can afford a private chef, now is the time to make the mistakes. Just say, "I am going to put these two ingredients together and see what the flavor is . . ." That's how it all started for me.

I once read about a successful businessman named John Chou. He described how a business was like an orchestra. It established my thoughts on how a meal is like an orchestra, too. The chef is the conductor, and each component on the plate represents a different sound. In order for the musical piece to be great, the flavors must be in harmony. But you won't know what works until you try. My hope is that the recipes here will inspire you to put on your apron, call the boys and lucky girls, get behind the stove, and cook.

This is just the beginning. Take the leap and see how easy and enjoyable cooking can be . . .

There is nothing more annoying than finding out you are missing a number of key ingredients for a recipe. Rather than having to always go back and forth to the super-market, there are a number of core items that should always be in your fridge and pantry.

Herbs & Spices

Basil
Cinnamon
Coriander
Cumin
Oregano
Rosemary
Salt and black pepper
Thyme

Protein

Almonds
Chicken breasts
    (freezer)
Chuck steak (freezer)
Eggs
Ground beef (freezer)
Ham
Walnuts

Fruits & Vegetables

Apples
Asparagus
Avocados
Bananas
Broccoli
Frozen berries
Garlic
Ginger
Green beans
Lemons
Long red chiles
Onions
Red and green bell
    peppers
Sweet potatoes
Tomatoes
Zucchini

Pantry

Chicken stock
Coconut milk
Fish sauce
Honey
Mustard
Soy sauce
Olive/Macadamia oil*

Grains & Beans

Brown rice
Red kidney beans
Rolled oats
Whole wheat pasta

Dairy

Grass-fed butter
Milk
Plain yogurt

---

* These two oils, when combined, are ideal for frying proteins and vegetables at high heats.

INGREDIENTS TO ALWAYS HAVE ON HAND . . .

Quality Knives

There is a saying that goes something like, "A good trades-man never blames his tools." In a cook's case, he or she can. If you have a bad knife, it will affect your cutting accuracy. Most important, it can cause serious injuries. Be sure to pick up a quality knife set—I use Global knives as I know they will literally cut my prep time in half.

Skillet (Frying Pan)

The difference between a good pan and a bad one is the cleaning time. A quality skillet doesn't take as long to clean up. So if you are on a budget, be prepared to stay at the sink for a little longer.

Oven

It doesn't have to be the biggest one in the world. I have worked with an oven that was so small it was also used as a stovetop. Learning to use your oven opens up a lot of new cooking opportunities.

Wooden Spoon

You can just use an ordinary cutlery spoon to mix and stir as you cook; however, a wooden spoon has a greater surface area and allows you to stir through bigger portions.

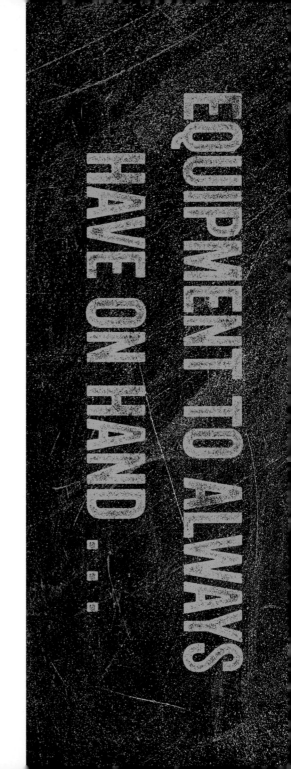

EQUIPMENT TO ALWAYS HAVE ON HAND . . .

Cutting Board

Make sure to use a wooden cutting board, as well as a white board for meat; anything else will ruin your blades.

Grater

A lot of preparations require produce, like ginger and garlic, to be grated. You can pick up graters that allow for a number of different cut sizes. Check them out at your local kitchen goods store.

Saucepan

If you're cooking soup, boiling water, or making sauces, you need a saucepan. Start off with a medium-size one, particularly if you are just looking after yourself. If you have the cash, purchasing a saucepan set will save you money in the long run, as they will come in all shapes and sizes.

Food Processor

Of all the things on this list, a food processor would be the least important. However, it can save you prep time and in the long run, it is a worthy investment. From experience, don't go cheap. But you can find some affordable handheld blenders that will do the job fine.

FOODS THAT LAST

The typical male eats a lot. And we can lack a bit of common sense when it comes to preparing weekly meals. One way to save time and money is to cook meals in bigger portions, so that they can be consumed over the course of the week. Admittedly, this may mean you have to plan ahead a few days, but it is much easier than it sounds. For example, when my week is particularly hectic, I cook a big, long-lasting meal on my quiet Mondays, which I can eat then and again later in the week for dinner or lunch when I am particularly time-poor. This is an effective method for all you "tight-arses," plus, I get to have my Spag Bol (page 27) more than once, or even twice, in the one week . . . win!

TIP: The secret to this recipe is to cook all the filling ingredients until they are three-quarters done. This prevents them from being overdone when they are baked.

CHICKEN AVO PIE

Serves 4

INGREDIENTS

1 large sweet potato, peeled and cut into 3/4-inch
    cubes
1 tablespoon olive/macadamia oil
1/4 pounds boneless, skinless chicken breast,
    chopped
1 onion, finely chopped
4 garlic cloves, crushed and chopped
2 1/2 cups trimmed green beans
1 cup sliced mushrooms
1 tablespoon dried tarragon

2 teaspoons dried thyme
1 cup chicken stock
1/3 cup white wine
1/2 cup coconut milk
1/4 cup grated tasty cheese (like cheddar), plus extra
    for sprinkling (optional)
1 avocado, pitted, peeled, and sliced
2 sheets puff pastry
1 regular egg, beaten

Preheat the oven to 425°F.

Place the sweet potato in a saucepan with enough water to cover. Bring to a boil and cook the sweet potato until just soft. Use a skewer to check—if it goes through with little resistance, it is perfect. Drain and allow to cool.

In a skillet, heat the oil over medium heat. Add the chicken and cook until lightly golden on all sides. Remove the chicken and add the onion and garlic to the pan; cook until lightly golden. Add the green beans and continue to stir for 2 minutes more. Return the chicken to the pan and add the cooked sweet potato, mushrooms, tarragon, and thyme. Continue to stir as you add the stock and cook for 1 minute more before adding the wine and coconut milk. Reduce the heat to low and simmer for 10 minutes. Gradually add the cheese. This mixture can then be refrigerated and used at a later time, i.e., if you come back late from work.

Divide the mixture evenly among ovenproof hot-pot bowls and top with the avocado slices. Sprinkle with extra cheese, if you'd like, and cover with the puff pastry. Using your knife, trim the pastry, making sure to leave a 1-inch overhang on all sides. Press the pastry against the edge of the bowl to seal. Using a fork, prick the pastry to allow steam to escape. Brush the pastry with egg and bake for 30 minutes.

CHICKEN CURRY
Serves 6

INGREDIENTS

2 cups basmati rice

1 tablespoon olive/macadamia oil

4 boneless, skinless chicken breasts, chopped

2 tablespoons red curry paste

4 shallots, sliced

1 tablespoon lemon juice

1 tablespoon fish sauce

1 2/3 cups chicken stock

1 bunch asparagus, ends trimmed, stalks sliced

1 1/2 cups coconut milk

Handful of trimmed green beans

Handful of trimmed snow peas

6 bok choi leaves, sliced

1 teaspoon freshly grated nutmeg

1/2 handful of bean sprouts

1/4 cup chopped fresh cilantro

In a saucepan, combine the rice and 2 1/2 cups water. Bring to a boil (the water will be very bubbly), then reduce the heat to low (close to "off" on the dial). Set the lid on a slight angle on top of the saucepan, allowing a small amount of steam to escape. Simmer for 12 to 15 minutes, until the rice is soft but still sticks together.

Heat a wok or a large saucepan over medium heat and add the oil. Add the chicken and cook for 2 minutes, then remove from the heat, making sure not to completely cook the chicken, as it will be returned to the pan later (you don't want it too tough).

Add more oil and stir in the red curry paste; cook, stirring, for 1 minute. Add the shallots and cook until brown. Mix in the lemon juice, fish sauce, stock, and asparagus. Bring to a boil, return the chicken to the pan, cover, and reduce the heat to medium-low. Simmer for 15 to 20 minutes.

Add the coconut milk, green beans, snow peas, bok choi, and nutmeg and stir before covering for another 5 minutes.

Serve with the rice, bean sprouts, and cilantro.

SLOW-ROASTED BEEF
Serves 4

Serve with Sweet Potato Patties (page 24).

INGREDIENTS

3 tablespoons olive/macadamia oil

2 1/4 pounds chuck steak, fat trimmed, cut into 1-inch pieces

2 onions, roughly chopped

2 tablespoons all-purpose flour

1 1/3 cups red wine

1 1/4 cups beef stock

Leaves from 2 sprigs fresh rosemary

3 bay leaves

Salt and black pepper

Handful of fresh flat-leaf parsley, roughly chopped

Preheat the oven to 350°F.

In a Dutch oven (a large, heavy-duty lidded cast-iron pot that is perfect for slow-cooking), heat 2 tablespoons of the oil over medium-high heat. In batches, cook the meat until golden brown (don't cook it all the way through—it must be still red on the inside, as it will cook again in the oven). Remove and set aside. Add the remaining 1 tablespoon of oil to the pot. Add the onions and cook until golden brown, 5 to 7 minutes. Add the flour and stir for another minute before adding the meat, wine, stock, rosemary, and bay leaves. Bring to a boil, season to taste with salt and pepper, cover, and put in the oven for 2 hours (the goal is for the meat to pull away in strips).

Using two forks, shred the meat. If it is cooked well, it will separate easily.

TIP: Always read the recipe first (e.g., this needs to cook for 2 hours, so plan ahead).

TIP: When slow-roasting meat, the cut you choose is very important. Cuts closer to joints have plenty of connective tissue, which breaks down when cooked. This makes the meat amazingly tender. When selecting a cut to slow-roast, choose one such as the shoulder—it melts in your mouth if cooked well.

INGREDIENTS

2 large sweet potatoes, peeled and chopped

3 1/2 tablespoons dairy or almond milk

2 tablespoons olive/macadamia oil, plus extra as needed

3 garlic cloves, finely chopped

1 regular egg

Place the sweet potatoes in a large saucepan with enough water to cover. Bring to a boil over high heat and cook for 6 to 8 minutes, until the potatoes are soft (check for doneness using a skewer). Drain the water and return the potatoes to the saucepan. Add the milk and 2 tablespoons of oil and mash until soft. Add the garlic and transfer to a bowl to cool.

Stir in the egg, which will hold the patties together. Using your hands, form the mixture into 12 patties and set aside.

Heat oil in a skillet over medium-high heat. Add the sweet potato patties, and using a spatula, flatten the patties down to 3/8 inch thick. Try to keep them in the shape of a circle; if they start to fall apart, simply play Mr. Fix-It and use a spoon to mold them back into shape. Cook on each side for 2 minutes or until lightly golden brown.

Use the sweet potato patties as a base and spoon some Slow-Roasted Beef on top. Serve with steamed greens.

TIP: Chop fresh herbs just before adding them to a dish to maximize their flavor.

SPAG BOL (SPAGHETTI BOLOGNESE)
Serves 3 or 4 hungry blokes

This is by far the most common meal known to mankind. If a guy has attempted to cook any dish, it should have been this. It is one of the easiest to prepare and has a lot of variations found not only in Italy but throughout the world. It is no surprise that this is my favorite for both lunch and dinner!

INGREDIENTS

4 garlic cloves, finely chopped

1 tablespoon olive/macadamia oil

1 onion, finely chopped

2 1/4 pounds premium ground beef

1 (14-ounce) can tomato puree

1 (14-ounce) can tomatoes

2 tablespoons tomato paste

Handful of fresh basil, finely chopped

1/2 handful of fresh oregano, finely chopped

1 (1-pound) package plain or whole wheat pasta

Grated Parmesan cheese, for serving

Before putting the saucepan on the heat, place the garlic in the pan and add a little bit of the oil, just enough so the garlic soaks it up. This allows the garlic flavor to infuse and spread throughout the sauce with the oil. Set the pan over high heat and cook the garlic for a minute before adding the rest of the oil and the onion. Stir until the onion is golden brown.

Next, brown the ground beef in batches, breaking up any big chunks with a spoon. Once the meat has browned, add the tomato puree, tomatoes, tomato paste, basil, and oregano. Stir until well combined. Reduce the heat to low and put a lid on the pan. Simmer, stirring occasionally, for 40 minutes. If you have the time, you can let it simmer for longer, which allows for a richer tomato flavor. The longer you simmer, the more the sauce infuses the meat.

While the sauce is cooking, bring a saucepan of water to a boil. Add the pasta, stir, and cook for 10 minutes. (Keep in mind that if you are using fresh pasta, it will only take 60 seconds.) Drain and set aside.

Remove the lid covering the sauce and raise the heat to medium-high. The lid stops all the moisture from escaping, so you end up with a very liquid sauce. If you prefer this consistency, take the lid off and let the sauce cook down for only 5 minutes before stirring in the pasta. For a thicker sauce, take the lid off and cook for 10 to 12 minutes before adding the pasta—use your own judgment. When ready, use tongs to stir in the pasta, then divide the pasta among 4 plates.

Serve with a badass healthy serving of the sauce and some grated Parmesan cheese.

SANDWICHING THE GYM

Going to the gym is pointless if you do not consume the right nutrients around your workouts. Your exercise goals are 30 percent based on your workouts—the other 70 percent involves what you are putting into your body. Your food has implications for your hormones, enzymes, and many molecules and systems that are required for the orderly function of your body. If you are a guy who is struggling to put on weight and is using the gym more than his mother's wallet, it comes down to your intake.

After a workout, your muscles tear as a result of repetitive contractions. Many people are confused and believe the reason they can't sit on a toilet after a workout is the result of too much work; however, the soreness comes from the repairing stage. Your body uses protein to repair the torn muscle fibers, and this causes what is called Delayed Onset of Muscle Soreness (DOMS). It is also important to consume protein, the macronutrient required for muscle repair, at the right times for muscle growth and adaptation. What's more, research shows that, post-exercise, the body needs some carbohydrates with the protein for optimal benefit. Carbs aid in the transportation process and with the work being carried out directly by the muscles.

Therefore, if you were to consume a protein meal versus a protein/carb meal, the latter will yield greater improvements in muscular adaptation. The following recipes have been formulated to ensure you have something to come home to in times of serious muscle repair. Your food is so important—just remember, your body is an indication of what you put into it.

CHOC-BANANA PROTEIN SHAKE

Makes 1 shake

The simplest recipe, and one that shows why having a blender is so useful.

INGREDIENTS

1 banana

1/4 cup LSA mix (see Tip)

1 scoop chocolate protein powder

1 cup almond milk

2 teaspoons chia seeds

1 teaspoon ground cinnamon

Combine all the ingredients in a blender and blend until smooth.

TIP: LSA stands for linseed (flaxseed), sunflower seed, and almond. It is great for your digestion and an amazing way to clean your insides.

TIP: You can add more flavor by simply changing the wraps from plain to spinach or tomato and herb, which are also found in the same location in the supermarket.

HERBED CHICKEN WRAP

Makes 8 wraps

These are a perfect lunchtime meal, and, if you don't have friends around, you can store them in the fridge for another day. A perfect example of planning ahead.

INGREDIENTS

Juice of 1/2 lemon

1 teaspoon dried thyme

1 teaspoon dried oregano

1 teaspoon dried marjoram

Salt and black pepper

1 3/4 pounds boneless, skinless chicken breast, diced

2 tablespoons extra-virgin olive oil, plus extra as needed

1 medium sweet potato, peeled and cut into small cubes

1 avocado, pitted, peeled, and sliced

8 wraps (found in the supermarket bread aisle)

Low-fat cottage cheese

Handful of arugula

In a bowl, mix the lemon juice, thyme, oregano, and marjoram with a pinch of salt and pepper. Add the chicken to the bowl and toss to coat.

In a skillet, heat 1 tablespoon of the oil over high heat. Add the chicken and cook until tender, 2 to 3 minutes. Transfer the chicken to a plate.

Add the remaining 1 tablespoon of the oil to the same pan. Add the sweet potato, sprinkle with some salt and pepper, and stir until the cubes are soft, 5 to 6 minutes. You may need to add a little more oil as you go depending on your pan. This will help transfer more heat to the cubes.

Divide the avocado evenly among the wraps. Place 2 teaspoons of cottage cheese on top, along with a handful of arugula. Next, evenly divide the sweet potato and chicken among the wraps.

Fold the two ends of the wrap together and then roll the wrap up like a burrito, tucking the sides in as you go. You can either have it as-is or put it in a sandwich press for 2 minutes to toast it. Alternatively, you can also toast it under the broiler.

SUMMER BEEF ROAST

Makes enough to share with 5 mates

INGREDIENTS

1 large sweet potato, peeled and chopped

2 parsnips, peeled and chopped

1/4 butternut squash, peeled, seeded, and chopped

2 Spanish onions, quartered

5 garlic cloves, left whole

Olive/macadamia oil

Salt and black pepper

Handful of fresh rosemary, roughly chopped

1 2/3 pounds rib eye fillet

1 tablespoon Dijon mustard

4 sprigs fresh thyme, or 1 tablespoon dried thyme

3 tablespoons balsamic vinegar

Preheat the oven to 375°F.

Place the sweet potato, parsnips, squash, onions, and garlic in a baking dish. Generously cover with 3 tablespoons of oil, sprinkle with salt and pepper to taste and the rosemary, then roast for 1 hour.

Truss the beef with cooking twine so it cooks evenly.

In a large skillet, heat 1 tablespoon of oil over high heat. Add the mustard, thyme, and balsamic vinegar and mix, then add the beef to the pan. Rotate the meat so that the outside is well browned, cooking for 1 to 2 minutes on each side. You want to brown the outside without cooking the center (which will be done in the oven).

Once the outside is completely browned, transfer the beef to a roasting pan and roast for 1 hour. Transfer the meat to a cutting board, cover with aluminum foil, and let rest for 5 minutes. Cut the string that was used to truss the beef and cut the meat into 1/2-inch-thick slices.

Serve with the vegetables and pan juices from the meat.

TIP: Do not discard the juice left in the roasting pan. Instead, transfer it to a saucepan with 2 tablespoons red wine and 2 tablespoons beef stock and cook over medium heat. This makes a beautiful sauce to pour over the meat.

TIP: Add a little fanciness by using a mold to plate the mash. Put the mash in a cup and pat it down. Grab a plate and place it upside down on top of the cup. Carefully turn both the cup and plate over. Shake the cup carefully and lift up to reveal the mash in the mold of a cup.

INGREDIENTS

The Sirloin . . .

1/3 cup soy sauce

1 tablespoon Dijon mustard

1/3 cup rice wine vinegar

1/3 cup Worcestershire sauce

4 (8-ounce) sirloin steaks

The Mash . . .

1 cup peas

1 teaspoon fresh chives, chopped

2 garlic cloves, finely chopped

1 tablespoon olive/macadamia oil

1 tablespoon sour cream

To marinate the steak, in a large flat dish, combine the soy sauce, mustard, vinegar, and Worcestershire sauce and stir. Place the steaks in the dish and move the meat around so that the marinade gets in everywhere. Cover with plastic wrap and put in the fridge until ready to cook. The longer you leave the meat in the marinade, the stronger the flavor will be. Overnight is ideal, but if you are pressed for time, 30 minutes will work (I have even done it in 15).

To make the mash, place the peas in a small saucepan with enough water to cover. Bring to a boil and cook for 6 minutes, or until the peas are really soft.

Drain the peas and transfer them to the bowl of a food processor. Add the chives, garlic, oil, sour cream, and one tablespoon of oil and pulse until the mixture is smooth. Set aside for serving. (Try to keep a lid on the food processor bowl or cover it with aluminum foil to keep the mash hot. The more times you make this, the better you will learn to cook the meat at the same time to serve together. Practice makes perfect.)

To cook the steaks, bring the steaks out of the fridge and let stand for 20 minutes to come to room temperature. In a grill pan or skillet, heat the remaining one tablespoon of oil over high heat. Place the steaks in the pan (you should hear a really nice sizzle) and cook, turning it every 15 seconds. When you flip the steaks, try to align the grill marks with any previous ones. For medium-rare, cook until the center of the meat springs back with the same resistance as when you touch your index finger and thumb together and poke that plump patch underneath your thumb (as always, the best marker is practice ☺).

Serve the steaks with the warm mash alongside.

TIP: WPI stands for whey protein isolate. It is simply a protein blend without any carbs, and a bit of flavoring. Most brands of protein powder have this type of formula. If you don't have it, it is not essential.

PROTEIN BROWNIES

Makes one 9 by 9-inch brownie slab . . . share at will

Enjoy these with the boys after a workout session, or with a girl who knows how important it is to have protein for recovery in her intake. ☺

INGREDIENTS

1/2 cup quality cacao powder, or 1/2 cup whole cacao beans

1/2 cup coconut oil, chilled if necessary to solidify

1/2 teaspoon ground cinnamon

1/2 cup coconut milk

3 tablespoons honey

1/2 cup WPI protein powder (see Tip)

1/2 cup almond meal

1 regular egg

Cocoa powder, for dusting

1/2 handful of crushed walnuts (optional)

1/2 handful of crushed macadamia nuts (optional)

Preheat the oven to 325°F. Line a 9-inch-square baking pan with parchment paper (this prevents the brownies from sticking).

If using cacao beans, place them in the bowl of a food processor and process until ground into a fine powder.

Combine the cacao powder (or ground beans), coconut oil, and cinnamon in a bowl. Using the back of a fork, break down the oil with the other ingredients until the mixture has the texture of bread crumbs. Add the coconut milk, honey, WPI protein powder, almond meal, and egg and stir.

Spoon the mixture into the prepared baking pan and using the back of the spoon, smooth out the top. Bake for 18 minutes, then insert a skewer into the center of the brownie block (this is the section that is the last to cook). If the skewer comes out clean with a few crumbs, it is done. If not, bake the brownies for 2 minutes more. Let cool completely before transferring to the fridge for 60 minutes.

Cut the brownie into portions. The brownie's center should be like the next girl . . . soft at heart. It will melt in your mouth.

Dust the brownies with cocoa powder and, if you are really keen, more WPI protein powder.

THE HANGOVER CURE

How about those mornings when you have that woodpecker constantly pounding your head, your mouth feels like it is filled with cotton balls, and you don't know whether to set up a bed next to the toilet . . .

These meals are formulated to get your body back into its right state. The cure varies from person to person—every individual has their own preferences. Some like it sweet, others prefer grease. Whatever your cure, this section is sure to help your Sunday be a little more enjoyable. The more you hydrate, the better you'll feel. These recipes include micronutrients that help you hold water for longer, and they are sure to somewhat aid in your hydration levels. Studies also show that having food in your stomach helps prevent a serious hangover; however, be sure to eat only once you are done letting everything else out.

TIP: The frozen yogurt can be fresh, or you can purchase some in advance and store it in the freezer. It is better frozen, as it melts onto the warm surface of the French toast.

BERRY COMPOTE FRENCH TOAST WITH CARAMEL SAUCE Serves 2 hungover fellas

INGREDIENTS

1 cup frozen mixed berries

1 tablespoon brown sugar

1 teaspoon ground cinnamon

4 regular eggs

Big soft white bread loaf, cut into 1-inch-thick slices

2 tablespoons unsalted butter

1 cup superfine sugar

1 teaspoon vanilla extract

3/4 cup light cream

3/4 cup plain frozen yogurt (vanilla or mixed berry works, too)

1/2 cup strawberries, chopped (optional)

salt and black pepper

Place the frozen mixed berries, 1 tablespoon of water, and 1/2 tablespoon of the brown sugar in a saucepan over low to medium heat. Cover and cook, stirring occasionally, for 8 to 10 minutes.

On a plate, mix the cinnamon and the remaining 1/2 tablespoon of brown sugar.

Whisk the eggs in a bowl and season with the salt and pepper. Dip the bread in, turning to ensure both sides are soaked. Grease a skillet with butter and set over medium-high heat. When it starts to bubble, place the bread in the pan. Cook the bread on each side for 1 minute and be sure not to burn it. Once cooked, immediately transfer to the plate with the brown sugar and cinnamon mixture. Turn to cover each side, then place on a serving plate.

Check on the berry compote. If it is still quite liquidy, raise the heat to high and remove the lid. (This is called reducing and it works by evaporating the water.) Once smooth in texture, remove from the heat and set aside.

In a saucepan, combine the superfine sugar and 1/3 cup of water and cook over low heat until the sugar dissolves (use a brush to remove any crystals that form on the sides of the pan). Raise the heat to medium-high, watching carefully for the mixture to turn golden brown (it can turn very quickly, so don't look away, or it will burn). Remove from the heat and stir in the cream—be careful, as the cream will sputter and release steam. Return the pan to the stovetop and keep warm, covered, over low heat until ready to serve.

To serve, cover the toast with the berry compote and top with yogurt before drizzling the caramel sauce over the top and adding the strawberries.

BREKKIE ON THE GO
Serves 1

INGREDIENTS

1 cup steel-cut or rolled oats
1/2 tablespoon plain yogurt (optional)
4 fresh strawberries, sliced
Handful of raspberries (fresh or frozen)
1/2 handful of fresh blueberries (optional)

1/2 handful of walnuts, chopped
3/4 tablespoon honey
1 teaspoon ground cinnamon
1 tablespoon WPI protein powder (see Tip, page 40; optional)

Place the oats and 1 cup of water in a saucepan (the water should just cover the oats) over medium to high heat. Stir until the mixture becomes thick (if you are really short for time, combine the water and oats in a bowl and place in the microwave for 2 minutes).

Take the mixture off the heat and place in a bowl. Add yogurt (if using) and stir through. Once well mixed, stir in the berries, walnuts, honey, cinnamon, and WPI protein powder (if using).

TIP: This is a great, healthy meal to have in the car on the way to work. It contains carbohydrates and protein to provide energy and muscle interaction for the day and is also a great source of omega-3s. The cinnamon even helps to speed up your metabolism, which is particularly important for those boys looking to improve that six-pack. The oat mixture can be made in bulk and the berries and nuts can be prepared in advance, just to save that extra time. By adding the WPI protein blend, you can have this as a pre-workout meal that is particularly great for those hitting the gym in the early hours of the morning.

PIZZA IN A PAN
Serves 2

INGREDIENTS

5 regular eggs

2 tablespoons olive/macadamia oil

1/2 onion, finely chopped

1 (10-ounce) boneless, skinless chicken breast or thigh, cut into 1-inch pieces

8 grape or cherry tomatoes, halved

1 teaspoon fresh rosemary, finely chopped

Salt and black pepper

Pesto (see page 93)

1/2 avocado, pitted, peeled, and sliced

1 (1 1/2 by 1/2-inch) feta block

Beat the eggs with a whisk or fork until completely combined. When lifting the fork or whisk out of the bowl, the egg should run off and not fall down in parts.

In a skillet, heat 1 tablespoon of the oil over high heat. Add the onion and cook until it begins to brown. Add the chicken and cook all the way through, 3 to 5 minutes. Transfer the chicken and onions to a plate.

Place the tomatoes and rosemary, along with a pinch of salt and pepper, in the same pan and cook for 1 minute; the tomatoes should begin to go quite soft. Transfer the tomatoes to a bowl.

Put the remaining 1 tablespoon of oil in the same pan and add half of the beaten eggs. Cook for 90 seconds. The egg will start to harden and little bubbles should start to rise to the surface. Carefully run a spatula underneath the egg base to loosen the edges.

Top the egg base like a pizza, using some pesto for the sauce and then distributing half the chicken, tomatoes, avocado, and feta over the top. Continue to slide the spatula underneath the egg so it does not stick to the surface of the pan. Cook until the bubbles on the surface of the egg base are set, then transfer to a plate. Repeat with the remaining egg, and top with the pesto and the remaining chicken, tomatoes, avocado, and feta to make a second "pizza."

INGREDIENTS

4 slices white bread
4 slices bacon
1 1/2 tablespoons butter
2 regular eggs

1 regular tomato, sliced
1/2 handful of fresh basil
1/3 cup grated tasty cheese (like cheddar)
Sliced bell pepper

Using the point of a knife, carefully cut out a circle 1 inch in diameter from the center of each slice of bread (if you have a glass or another circular object with the same diameter, this can also be used). If you don't put too much pressure on the bread, you can stack the slices and cut circles from two at the same time.

Place the bacon in a medium saucepan and cook until crispy, no more than 2 minutes on each side. Transfer to a plate once cooked.

Melt the butter over medium to high heat. Place the bread in the pan and cook until toasted and golden brown (if the pan is too small for two slices, do one at a time, using one-fourth of the butter for each). Carefully crack an egg into the hole in one slice of bread. Run a spatula underneath the bread to ensure the egg and the bread don't stick to the pan.

Cook the egg on the first side for 90 seconds before flipping it onto the other side to cook for 1 minute more. If it's not ready, the egg will be too runny to flip and won't hold its shape; if the yolk is still runny but the white is set you cooked it perfectly (this may take a few attempts to master).

Preheat the broiler. Remove the bread from the pan and set it on a baking sheet. Place the bacon, tomato, basil leaves, and cheese (reserve a bit for sprinkling) on top of one slice of the bread. Stack the other slice on top, sprinkle with the reserved cheese, and broil it until the cheese on top has melted.

INSIDE-OUT SPICY OMELET

Serves 1

INGREDIENTS

1 tablespoon olive/macadamia oil, plus extra as
  needed
1 slice ham, thinly sliced (off the bone is best)
2 regular eggs
1 teaspoon red pepper flakes
1/2 teaspoon ginger, finely grated

1 teaspoon crumbled feta cheese
4 cherry tomatoes, halved
Handful of baby spinach
1 tablespoon balsamic vinegar, plus extra for serving
Salt and black pepper

In a skillet, heat the oil over medium-high heat. Carefully place the ham in the pan and cook for 2 minutes, until it begins to turn crispy. Turn over and cook for 1 minute more. Transfer the ham to a plate lined with parchment paper.

In a bowl, whisk together the eggs, red pepper flakes, and ginger until well combined. Pour the egg mixture into the pan in which you cooked the ham, and add the feta cheese. Using a spatula, fold the egg as it cooks so that it becomes scrambled. Do not let the egg settle for too long on the surface of the pan or it will overcook and become too dry. When the egg still looks soft but holds together, transfer it to the plate with the ham, plating it on top of the ham.

Add some more oil to the pan, then add the tomatoes and cook for 2 minutes before adding the spinach and balsamic vinegar and cooking for 1 minute more.

To serve, grabbing the parchment paper, roll the ham over the top of the egg. Be mindful, as the egg can fall out of the sides (if this happens, you can use it for presentation). Spoon the spinach on top and then the tomatoes. Season with the salt and pepper and drizzle oil and vinegar around the edges.

BASIC BRO BURGER

Makes 4 burgers.

INGREDIENTS

The Chutney . . .

4 tomatoes, halved
4 garlic cloves
2 sprigs fresh rosemary
Olive-macadamia oil
2 teaspoons brown sugar or rice
    malt syrup
1/4 cup balsamic vinegar

The Burgers . . .

1 pound premium ground beef
1/2 bunch of flat-leaf parsley,
    chopped
1/2 bunch of fresh cilantro,
    chopped
1 onion, finely chopped
1 regular egg

Tasty cheese slices
4 whole-grain hamburger buns
Garlic Aioli (page 79)
Handful of arugula
1 avocado

To make the chutney, preheat the oven to 350°F.

Place the tomatoes, garlic, and rosemary on a baking sheet and drizzle with oil. Bake for 8 minutes, then transfer to a blender and pulse to create a tomato sauce.

Transfer the tomato sauce to a saucepan and cook over medium heat, stirring, for a minute before adding the brown sugar and vinegar. Continue to stir for 1 minute more, then cover the pan, reduce the heat to low, and simmer the chutney for 6 minutes.

To make the burgers, in a large bowl, mix together the ground beef, parsley, cilantro, onion, and egg until well combined. Using your hands, divide the beef mixture into four portions and form them into large balls.

In a saucepan, heat one tablespoon of oil over high heat. Working in batches if necessary, place the balls in the pan and flatten them with the back of a spatula to create patties about 1 inch thick. The meat should sizzle. Cook for 3 minutes on the first side before turning over. Place a slice of cheese on top of each burger and cook on the second side for 2 minutes.

Heat a grill pan over medium to high heat. Cut the buns in half and place them in the pan. Cook until toasted but not burned, no more than 30 seconds.

For each burger, spread some garlic aioli on the cut side of one bun half and place a handful of arugula on top. Stack the patty over the arugula, cheese-side up, and then spoon some tomato chutney on top. Finish by spreading some avocado onto the other half of the bun, top the burger, and try to fit a whole bite in your mouth at once.

CUT YOUR CALORIES

Who would have thought DudeFood could be healthy? If you're looking to trim up, or boost your energy levels, this section is perfect for you. These meals have been developed to include the right macronutrients of protein and quality fats with minimal carbohydrates. It's important to have a balanced nutritional intake; however, with your body holding a 500-gram carbohydrate tank, your ability to see that six-pack can be impeded if you overdose on your starches (i.e., pasta and bread). Your ability to burn fat is maximized when your carb tank is empty, as your body then relies on fat as its primary source of fuel. Therefore, a low intake of carbs is important for weight loss.

The timing of your meals is also important. What do the majority of you boys do when you finish your dinner? Watch TV, browse Facebook . . . so, pretty much nothing. As a result, you are expending no energy before you go to bed. If you eat a high-carbohydrate meal at dinner, such as pasta, it means that in the morning you haven't burned off many of the carbs from that meal. You then have more carbs at breakfast, and the resulting effect is no burn-off of fat.

Have the majority of your carbs, such as your oats, etc., in the morning, and you will burn them off over the course of your active day. Toward 3 P.M., you should start to look toward your salads and meats and vegetables, which contain high levels of protein, micronutrients, and required fats. That said, your life should never be too regimented, especially when it comes to your food. There are times when someone might invite you out to dinner after work, and you should enjoy yourself.

(FRIGGIN') AMAZING SALAD

Serves 2

INGREDIENTS

3 garlic cloves, finely chopped

1 tablespoon soy sauce

1 tablespoon honey

1 1/4 pounds boneless, skinless chicken breast, cut into 1-inch pieces

2 big handfuls of arugula

Big handful of baby spinach

6 sun-dried tomatoes, sliced

1 (2 3/4 by 1/2-inch) feta block, thinly sliced

1 tablespoon olive/macadamia oil

Juice of 1/2 lemon

Handful of macadamia nuts (optional)

In a large bowl, mix the garlic, soy sauce, and honey until well combined. Add the chicken and use your hands to coat it with the marinade; set aside. Marinate for a minimum of 30 minutes, but overnight is best.

In a large salad bowl, toss together the arugula, spinach, sun-dried tomatoes, and feta.

In a skillet, heat the oil over medium to high heat. When it moves around the pan easily or starts to smoke, add the chicken and cook for 6 minutes, or until cooked through. (To test, cut through the center of a piece, and if it is still pink, cook it longer. It is perfect if the meat is quite squishy but white in the center.) Pull it off the heat straightaway.

Add the chicken and the lemon juice to the bowl with the arugula mixture and toss to combine. Serve as-is or topped with some macadamias, if you like.

CHICKEN STIR-FRY WITH BROWN BASMATI RICE Serves 4

INGREDIENTS

1 1/2 cups brown basmati rice (you can use white basmati if brown is not available)

1 teaspoon sesame oil

1 1/4 pounds boneless, skinless chicken breast, cut into 1-inch cubes

1 tablespoon olive/macadamia oil

3 garlic cloves, finely chopped

5 scallions, sliced

1 bunch asparagus, cut into 1 1/2-inch pieces

1 head broccoli, stem and crown chopped

1 zucchini, sliced

1/2 red bell pepper, seeded and sliced

Handful of green beans, ends trimmed

1 long red chile, seeded and finely chopped

1/3 cup chicken stock

1 1/2 tablespoons soy sauce

1 teaspoon grated fresh ginger

1/3 cup cashews

In a saucepan, combine the rice and a scant 2 cups of water. Bring to a boil (the water will be very bubbly) then reduce the heat to low (close to "off" on the dial). Set the lid on the pan at a slight angle, allowing a small amount of steam to escape. Simmer for 12 to 15 minutes, until the rice is soft but still sticks together.

In a skillet, heat half the sesame oil over medium heat. Working in batches, add the chicken and cook for 1 minute. Don't cook the chicken all the way through. Transfer the chicken to a bowl.

Add the oil, garlic, and scallions to the pan and stir for 30 seconds before adding the asparagus, broccoli, and zucchini. Cook, stirring, for 2 to 3 minutes more, or until the broccoli begins to soften. Next, add the bell pepper, green beans, chopped chile, and stock. Raise the heat to high and cook, stirring, for 2 minutes. Return the chicken to the pan along with the soy sauce and ginger and the remaining sesame oil. Continue to cook, stirring, for 1 to 2 minutes, until the chicken is cooked through (test by getting a big piece and cutting it in half—it should not be pink in the center). Add the cashews and cook for a final 30 seconds.

Serve the wickedly colorful and tasty stir-fry over the rice.

TIP: Microwaveable rice is great in a pinch. Just microwave it for 90 seconds and add a portion to your meal.

BISON HOISIN & GREENS

Serves 4, or 3 hungry boys

INGREDIENTS

2 cups brown rice

1 tablespoon sesame oil

4 scallions, thinly sliced

1 1/4 pounds bison fillet

2 teaspoons grated fresh ginger

1 long red chile, seeded and finely chopped

Handful of broad beans, ends trimmed

2 bunches broccolini (looks like the son of broccoli and asparagus), chopped

1 zucchini, halved lengthwise and cut into half-moons

1 bunch bok choi, stalks removed, leaves roughly chopped

1 green bell pepper, seeded and sliced

3/4 cup beef stock

2 tablespoons hoisin sauce

In a saucepan, combine the rice and 2 1/2 cups of water. Bring to a boil (the water will be very bubbly), then reduce the heat to low (close to "off" on the dial). Set the lid on the pan at a slight angle, allowing a small amount of steam to escape. Simmer for 12 to 15 minutes, until the rice is soft but still sticks together.

In a wok or large saucepan, heat the oil and the scallions over high heat. Be careful, as the oil will spit. Cook until golden, then add the bison and cook, stirring continuously, for just 1 minute. Transfer the bison to a plate. Add the ginger and chile to the pan and cook for 30 seconds. Stir in the broad beans, broccolini, and zucchini. Continue to cook, stirring, for 3 to 4 minutes, or until the broccolini begins to soften. Add the bok choi and bell pepper and cook, stirring, for 1 minute. Add the stock and reduce the heat to medium. Cook for 2 minutes more before returning the bison to the pan. Add the hoisin sauce and cook, stirring, for a final minute.

Serve the stir-fry in bowls with some of the brown rice.

TIP: Cut the green ends of the scallions on an angle. They make an awesome garnish to sprinkle over the top.

INGREDIENTS

2 teaspoons peanut oil

1 tablespoon grated fresh ginger

1 onion, finely chopped

2 1/4 pounds ground beef

1 zucchini, julienned (see Tip)

1 (8-ounce) can water chestnuts, drained

1 (8-ounce) can bamboo shoots, drained

2 long red chiles, finely chopped

2 tablespoons fish sauce

3 tablespoons oyster sauce

1/3 cup soy sauce

Large handful of bean sprouts

1 head iceberg lettuce, leaves separated and kept
   whole, for serving

Heat a wok or large skillet over high heat. Add the peanut oil and the ginger and cook, stirring, for 1 minute. Add the onion and cook, stirring, until golden. Add the beef and cook, stirring, until it has browned.

Add the zucchini, water chestnuts, bamboo shoots, and chiles and cook, stirring, for 1 minute. Add the fish sauce, oyster sauce, and soy sauce and mix well. Turn off the heat and stir the bean sprouts into the mixture before spooning it into the lettuce cups.

TIP: When you julienne, you cut the produce into long, matchstick-like shapes. First, cut the vegetable into thin slices, then cut the slices into skinny matchsticks about as wide as they are thick. The length is generally 2 inches.

MANGO & LEMON SORBET

Serves 3

Summer can be unbearable without some sort of treat to keep your taste buds tame. With only two ingredients, your friends will take longer to get their bowls out of the cupboard than it takes you to make this mango and lemon sorbet.

INGREDIENTS

2 cups frozen mango chunks
Zest and juice of 1 lemon
Plain yogurt (optional)

Place the ingredients in a blender and blitz until smooth. If you feel like a bit of a treat, add a bit of plain yogurt for a smoother consistency.

Scoop the sorbet into a bowl immediately to enjoy on a hot day, or spoon it into a container and freeze it to eat later.

FRUIT SOUP
Serves 3

INGREDIENTS

2 peaches, halved, pitted, and chopped

1 mango, pitted, peeled, and chopped

1 1/2 cups strawberries, chopped

Zest of 1 lime

Zest and juice of 1/2 lemon

1/2 cup frozen raspberries

1/2 teaspoon ground cinnamon

Seeds of 1 passion fruit

In a bowl, combine the peaches, mango, 1 cup of the strawberries, the lime zest, lemon zest, and lemon juice. Mix together and then add the frozen raspberries and cinnamon. Seal well with plastic wrap and refrigerate, ideally overnight. The longer you have the dish chilling, the better the flavor becomes.

Serve topped with the remaining strawberries and passion fruit seeds.

OVEN-BAKED PEACH SURPRISE

Makes 4

Serve with ice cream.

INGREDIENTS

1/4 cup macadamia nuts
1/4 cup walnuts
1/4 cup hazelnuts
2 peaches

2 tablespoons honey
1 teaspoon ground cinnamon
1/2 cup frozen raspberries

Preheat the oven to 350°F.

Put the macadamias, walnuts, and hazelnuts in a double-layered sandwich bag and use the edge of a rolling pin to lightly crush them. Be sure to not let off too much aggression, as you may burst the bag. The nuts should still be as solid as The Rock—if they look like bread crumbs, you don't need another gym session.

Cut the peaches in half lengthwise and, using a spoon, carefully pit them. If done correctly, you should have a nice "peach bowl" remaining.

Place the peaches on a baking sheet, cut side up. Take 1 1/2 tablespoons of the honey and half fill the "peach bowl" with honey, and then drizzle over the rest of the cut surface. Sprinkle with half the cinnamon and bake for 6 to 8 minutes, or until the peaches are a nice golden color.

In a skillet, dry roast (without oil) the crushed nuts over medium heat for 1 minute. Add the remaining 1/2 tablespoon honey, sprinkle with the remaining cinnamon, and cook, stirring, for 30 seconds. The mixture should start to bubble slowly and turn a caramel color.

Reduce the heat to low and continue to stir so the mixture does not go hard. If the mixture becomes too dark (it should stay golden), take the pan off the heat.

Take the peaches out of the oven and place a few raspberries in the "peach bowl," and then bake the peaches for 1 to 2 minutes more, or until the juice of the raspberries runs.

Remove from the oven and carefully add the caramelized nuts on top of the raspberries.

FINGER-LICKING FEEDS

It is no surprise that when you think of DudeFood, you likely think of mouth-watering, finger-licking feeds that ooze and drip a juicy mess! This section is full of meals requiring a number of napkins. They should only be made for a first date if you are very confident. They are great for a party, or to just have on a Sunday with the boys. One thing is guaranteed: You are sure to be surprised at just how easy cooking finger-licking feeds can be.

INGREDIENTS

1 tablespoon olive/macadamia oil

1/2 onion, finely chopped

3 garlic cloves, finely chopped

1/4 cup chopped ham

1/2 can red kidney beans

1/2 can chopped diced tomatoes

2 teaspoons red pepper flakes

1 tablespoon dried marjoram

2 regular eggs

Salt and black pepper

Olive Oil Pita Chips (page 99), for serving

Preheat the oven to 350°F.

In a skillet, heat the oil over high heat. Add the onion and sauté, stirring continuously, for 2 minutes. Add the garlic and continue to cook, stirring, until the onion is golden brown. Add the ham and cook until it begins to brown. Add the beans and tomatoes and sauté for 1 minute before adding the red pepper flakes and marjoram. Reduce the heat to low, cover, and simmer for 10 minutes.

Divide the sauce between two ramekins (small, round, ovenproof dishes) and flatten the tops evenly. Do not fill the ramekins all the way to the top, as you must allow room for the egg to cook and rise. Carefully crack an egg on top of the sauce in each ramekin, trying to keep the yolk intact. Bake for 6 to 8 minutes.

To check if they are done, shake the ramekin—the surface should still slightly jiggle.

To serve, top with salt and pepper. Dip your chips into the yolk and watch the yummy mess unfold!

TIP: Remember, food cooked in the oven continues to cook when you bring it out, so account for cooking time out of the oven and allow your food time to cool. If it's perfect right out of the oven, it may be overdone by the time it hits your mouth!

CHICKEN & HERB BALLS WITH GARLIC AIOLI

Makes 12 balls

INGREDIENTS

The Chicken Balls . . .

10 ounces boneless, skinless chicken breast, fat
   removed
Handful of fresh flat-leaf parsley, roughly chopped,
   plus more for serving
1/2 handful of fresh oregano, roughly chopped
1/2 handful of fresh cilantro, roughly chopped
3 1/2 tablespoons unsalted butter
1 (1 1/2-inch) cube Parmesan cheese, grated
1/2 long red chile, seeded and finely chopped
   (optional)
1 1/4 cups bread crumbs
2 tablespoons of olive/macadamia oil, for cooking

The Garlic Aioli . . .

1 egg yolk
2 garlic cloves
Juice of 1/2 lemon
1 teaspoon sugar
1 teaspoon Dijon mustard
Pinch of salt
Pinch of black pepper
1/3 cup extra-virgin olive oil

To make the chicken balls, combine all the chicken ball ingredients except the bread crumbs in the bowl of a food processor and process until the mixture resembles sticky dough. Using your hands, roll the mixture into balls about the size of a golf ball. Put the bread crumbs in a shallow dish and coat the balls in the bread crumbs. Set aside for 10 minutes.

Pour oil into a heavy saucepan on medium to high heat. Add the balls. Be careful—the oil may splatter. Turn continuously until the whole surface is golden brown, about 4 minutes . . . watch the cheese melt.

To make the aioli, combine all the aioli ingredients except the oil in a blender. With the blender running, gradually pour in the oil, allowing it to thicken the mixture into a sauce.

Serve the chicken balls in a bowl topped with extra parsley and the aioli.

HARISSA CHICKEN DRUMMIES WITH COOLING BASIL YOGURT
Serves 4 Super Bowl lovers

INGREDIENTS

1 long red chile, seeded and finely chopped

1 red bell pepper, ribs removed

1 onion, roughly chopped

1 garlic clove, roughly chopped

2 tablespoons olive or macadamia oil

Pinch of salt

1 tablespoon paprika

2 teaspoons ground cumin

2 teaspoons ground coriander

2 1/4 pounds chicken drumsticks

1/2 cup plain yogurt

Small handful of fresh basil, finely chopped

Juice of 1/2 lemon

Preheat the oven to 400°F. Line a baking sheet with parchment paper.

In a blender or food processor, combine the chile, bell pepper, onion, garlic, and oil, and blend until a paste is formed. Add the salt, paprika, cumin, and coriander and continue to blend until combined. Pour the mixture into a large bowl.

Add the drumsticks to the bowl with the blended mixture and stir with a spatula to coat. Spread the drumsticks in an even layer on the prepared baking sheet, then bake for 12 to 15 minutes, or until the meat is falling off the bones.

In a small bowl, stir together the yogurt, basil, and lemon juice and set aside until ready to serve.

Serve the chicken with the cooling yogurt, and enjoy. ☺

TIP: Quinoa is a healthy substitute for rice. It contains significantly less starch, but still has a large amount of fiber. It is high in protein and gluten-free. You can make the wrap without quinoa if you're in a hurry, but it's a fantastic ingredient to help fill you up. A good rule of thumb for cooking quinoa is to use 1 1/2 cups water to every 1 cup quinoa. Combine the quinoa and water in a saucepan, bring to a boil, then reduce the heat to low, set a lid ajar on top of the pan, and simmer for 10 minutes.

Makes 8 wraps, serves 3 hungry boys

Here is another "make in bulk" meal. These wraps are great to eat on the run, but feel free to add the meatballs to a salad or some roast veggies to mix it up. Once you make the meatballs, you are free to have them whatever way suits.

INGREDIENTS

1/2 cup quinoa
1 pound ground lamb
1 regular egg
1 teaspoon ground cumin
1/2 teaspoon fennel seeds, ground
4 splashes Tabasco sauce
3 tablespoons plain Greek yogurt
Zest and juice of 1 lime or lemon

1/2 cucumber, roughly chopped
2 teaspoons fresh mint, finely chopped
1 bunch flat-leaf parsley, roughly chopped
1 Spanish onion, roughly chopped
1 tablespoon olive/macadamia oil
4 flatbreads
Hummus (see page 97)

Cook the quinoa as directed on the package (see Tip) and allow to cool for 5 minutes.

In a large bowl, use your hands to combine the ground lamb, cumin, fennel, and Tabasco. Roll the mixture into balls about the size of a golf ball and set aside.

In a small bowl, combine the yogurt, lime zest, cucumber, and mint. In a separate large bowl, combine the parsley, onion, lime juice, and cooked quinoa; set aside.

In a skillet, heat the oil over high heat. Add the lamb balls and cook all over, turning frequently, until golden brown. The whole process should take 5 to 6 minutes. If you are struggling to keep them cooking evenly, roll the balls against each other or use the edge of the pan to hold them in place.

To serve, spread some hummus in the middle of a flatbread. On top, evenly divide the quinoa mixture into 8. Pile on 3 meatballs and spoon a dollop of the yogurt mixture over the top. Roll the flatbread like a burrito, tucking the sides as you go.

ZESTY CRUSTED FISH
Serves 1

Serve with Sweet Potato Strips (see page 86).

INGREDIENTS

1 teaspoon coriander seeds
1 teaspoon cumin seeds
1 teaspoon fennel seeds
Pinch of salt

Zest of 1/2 lemon
2 teaspoons olive/macadamia oil
1 (7-ounce) white fish fillet (pollock works well here)

Preheat the oven to 350°F.

In a small skillet, dry roast (without oil) the coriander, cumin, and fennel seeds over high heat for 60 to 90 seconds. Transfer to a mortar and pound with a pestle into a coarse, not fine, powder, then mix in salt and lemon zest.

In a large ovenproof skillet, heat the oil over high heat. Add the fish fillet and cook for 2 minutes, or until the fish turns opaque. Turn the fish over and generously sprinkle it with the spice mix. Transfer the pan to the oven and bake for 2 minutes, or until cooked throughout. To test, insert a knife into the thickest part of the fillet and then gently press it to your bottom lip. It should be warm. If it is cold, leave the fish in the oven for 1 minute more, and then test again.

SWEET POTATO STRIPS
Serves 2

INGREDIENTS

1 sweet potato, peeled
3 tablespoons olive/macadamia oil, plus extra as needed
Salt and black pepper

Using a vegetable peeler, cut the sweet potato into long strips. Repeat until just a knob of sweet potato remains.

Wrap the strips in a paper towel and carefully press down to get rid of any excess moisture. You may need to do this in batches.

In a skillet, heat the oil over high heat. This is not like deep-frying, it's shallow frying. Test the oil's temperature by adding a small piece of the sweet potato. If it bubbles straightaway, add a small handful of the strips and listen for the magic sizzle. Fry until the strips turn golden, 3 to 5 minutes, turning them to get nice caramelization on both sides. Transfer to a bowl lined with paper towels, and season with a pinch of salt and pepper. Repeat the process with the remaining strips. If the oil begins to darken or smoke, carefully discard it and start again with fresh oil.

Serve with the Zesty Crusted Fish (page 85).

GARLIC-BUTTER SHRIMP
Serves 4

INGREDIENTS

1 1/2 —2 pounds raw large shrimp

1/2 tablespoon extra-virgin olive oil

8 garlic cloves, thinly sliced

7 tablespoons grass-fed butter

4 fresh sage leaves

Zest and juice of 1/2 lemon

Salt

Handful of fresh flat-leaf parsley, chopped

To peel the shrimp, separate the head from the body at the neck, and then pull from the base of the legs. The shell should peel off the body in one or two sections. Make sure the tail section is intact. Using the pointy end of the knife blade, make a shallow, straight cut along the spine of the shrimp. This will unveil the shrimp's intestine line. Grasp the end of the dark vein between the pointy end of the blade and your thumb and carefully separate it from the flesh. Once removed, simply use your fingers to pull it from the shrimp's body and discard it.

In a saucepan, heat the oil over medium-high heat. Add the garlic and cook until it browns. Reduce the heat to medium, add the butter, and, when it has almost completely melted, add the sage leaves, lemon zest, and salt. Stir for 30 seconds before adding the shrimp. Cook for 1 to 2 minutes, or until the shrimp turn red or bright pink in color. Remove from the heat and stir in the lemon juice and parsley before serving.

SUPER SIDES

Just as for every Batman, there is a Robin, for every juicy piece of meat, there is an amazing side to offset its flavor and provide balance. These sides have been created to be used as a spread, filler, and flavor addition. It is a great idea to have a number of them in the fridge so you can mix and match between meals, and if you are running late, they can be used to add punch to some chicken or beef. These sides have been paired with a number of recipes, but use your imagination and palate and find out what other meals they work with. It is through these experiments that you learn the most about food.

There are a number of recipes in DudeFood *that require this pesto. Alter the measurements to get your own ideal flavor.*

INGREDIENTS

Handful of pine nuts
1 garlic clove
2 handfuls of fresh basil leaves

1/4 cup grated Parmesan cheese
Olive/macadamia oil

In a small skillet, dry roast (without oil) the pine nuts over medium heat until golden brown.

With a mortar and pestle, crush the garlic until well ground. Add the pine nuts and continue to crush until the mixture has the texture of bread crumbs.

Finely chop the basil. The finer, the better, as this releases its flavor. Add the basil to the garlic mixture and continue to crush. Add half the Parmesan.

Gradually pour in the oil. The amount of oil is up to you. If you like a drier mixture, then refrain from adding a lot. If you prefer a thicker paste, gradually add more. Continue to taste the pesto so that you can balance out the oil with the remaining Parmesan as needed.

STUFFED TOMATOES
Serves 6

INGREDIENTS

1 cup quinoa or brown rice

6 tomatoes

1 tablespoon ground cumin

2 tablespoons dried mixed herbs, or 1 teaspoon dried
   oregano and 1 teaspoon dried thyme

1 tablespoon olive/macadamia oil

Handful of grated Parmesan cheese

Preheat the oven to 390°F. Line a baking sheet with parchment paper.

In a saucepan, combine the quinoa and 2 cups of water. Bring to a boil over high heat, then reduce the heat to low, set a lid on the pan at a slight angle to allow steam to escape, and simmer for 10 minutes.

Slice the top off the tomatoes and, using a spoon, scoop the pulp and the seeds into a bowl. Set the hollowed-out tomatoes on the prepared baking sheet and set aside. Add the cumin and dried herbs to the bowl with the tomato pulp and seeds and stir.

In a medium skillet, heat the oil over medium-high heat. Add the tomato pulp mixture and cook for 5 to 7 minutes. Carefully transfer to a blender and pulse until pureed or, for those not familiar, really liquidy.

Pour the tomato mixture into a bowl, add the quinoa, and stir to combine. Spoon the quinoa filling into the empty tomato shells. Bake for 4 to 6 minutes. For extra flavor, sprinkle some Parmesan on top and bake for 1 minute more, or until the cheese turns a golden brown.

INGREDIENTS

The Chips . . .

1 parsnip, peeled and sliced, cut into rounds

1 1/2 tablespoons honey

7 tablespoons olive/macadamia/grapeseed oil, plus extra as needed

The Hummus . . .

1 (14-ounce) can chickpeas, drained and rinsed

2 garlic cloves, crushed

1 1/2 tablespoons fresh lemon juice

2 tablespoons tahini (sesame seed paste)

1 teaspoon paprika

Preheat the oven to 375°F.

Spread the parsnips in a single layer on a baking sheet. In a bowl, mix the honey and 2 tablespoons oil and pour over the parsnips. Use a spoon or tongs to mix the honey and oil throughout the parsnips so they're all well coated. Bake for 8 to 12 minutes, or until the parsnips are golden.

In the bowl of a food processor, combine the chickpeas, garlic, lemon juice, tahini, and paprika. With the processor running, gradually add the remaining 5 tablespoons of oil. If the hummus is too thick, add more oil or water until it reaches the consistency you desire.

Serve the hummus in a dip tray with the parsnip chips on the side.

OLIVE OIL PITA CHIPS

Serves 4

Seriously: With just two ingredients and a bit of seasoning, you have an amazing accompaniment for dips or nachos. Simple and quick. A great option for an afternoon barbecue with a beer.

INGREDIENTS

2 flatbreads
Extra-virgin olive oil
Salt and black pepper

Preheat the oven to 350°F.

Separate the flatbreads into single sheets, if necessary (sometimes the bread comes folded over, so cut it at the seam and separate). Cut the bread into mini pizza triangles, keeping in mind that the bigger they are, the more fragile they will be. Spread the bread pieces on a baking sheet and brush with oil. The amount is up to you. The more you add, the stronger the olive flavor will be. Sprinkle with some salt and pepper and bake for 2 to 3 minutes. Keep an eye on the chips—because they are thin, they will cook quickly. Carefully transfer the chips to a wire rack when they are done so they don't sweat against the pan as they cool.

FIRST DATE

Makes 9 balls

This is a great snack for an afternoon pick-me-up. Dates contain a lot of good antioxidants, which help rid the body of toxins and free radicals. These are sweet, so make sure you don't eat them all at once.

INGREDIENTS

1/2 cup pitted dried dates

1/4 cup shredded, unsweetened coconut, plus extra for dusting

1 teaspoon ground cinnamon

1/2 handful of walnuts, crushed with your hands

1/4 cup hazelnut meal (optional)

In the bowl of a food processor, combine all the ingredients and pulse until finely mixed together. Using your hands, roll the mixture into balls the size of golf balls. They should hold together, but you may need to give them a good squish. If you are really struggling, add more hazelnut meal or coconut.

Spread the extra shredded coconut on a plate and roll the date balls in the coconut to coat.

SQUASH BLOSSOMS
Makes 6

INGREDIENTS

3 tablespoons ricotta cheese

5 sun-dried tomatoes, finely chopped

1/2 handful of fresh oregano, finely chopped

2 regular eggs

1 tablespoon olive/macadamia oil

6 squash blossoms

In a small bowl, stir together the ricotta, tomatoes, and oregano. In a separate small bowl, whisk the eggs.

Carefully open the zucchini flowers and spoon an equal amount of the ricotta mixture into each. You can use your hands, and if the flower does break, you can easily pull a petal back over.

In a saucepan, heat the oil over high heat. Holding a zucchini flower by the stem, dip the flower end into the beaten egg, making sure it is well coated. Place the zucchini flower in the pan and repeat to coat the remaining flowers. Cook the stuffed flowers, turning them occasionally, for 1 to 2 minutes, or until the egg is cooked, then carefully transfer to a paper towel to drain.

Serve as a side or eat as-is.

FRESH PASTA
Serves 1

Cooking homemade pasta sounds so intimidating, but it is one of the easiest and most fulfilling foods to accomplish. Not only is fresh pasta cheaper than the packaged stuff, but it also tastes better and doesn't have additives and preservatives, which can be harmful to the body.

The simple rule behind pasta is 3/4 cup of flour to 1 egg. The poorer parts of Northern Italy relied on water as eggs were too expensive. Sometimes you may find that one egg is not enough; this is dependent on its size. I have found that one extra-large egg is just enough, but the humidity at the time can also affect the consistency of your pasta. Always have extra flour and eggs on hand to balance it out just in case the dough becomes too sticky or too dry.

INGREDIENTS

3/4 to 1 1/4 cups all-purpose flour, plus extra for dusting
1 to 2 extra-large eggs
1 1/2 tablespoons extra-virgin olive oil

Pour 3/4 cup of the flour onto a dry wooden cutting board. Using your fingers, make a well in the center and crack an egg into it, adding the oil at the same time. Using a fork, whisk the egg within the center of the flour, gradually mixing in the rim of the flour well. The egg mixture will start to look like a sticky dough.

This is the point where you get your hands dirty.

Dust your hands with flour and start to mix the rest of the flour into the egg mixture. At this point, try not to push the mixture down onto the cutting board, as it will stick. Using your palms, fold the mixture and push it forward, constantly turning the loose flour and getting it involved. This is where you make the call if the dough needs more flour. If it is still sticking to your hands, dust more flour down and fold it through. Continue to do this until you can roll the dough into a ball without it sticking to anything. It should feel soft and Play-Doh like. If it is rock hard, you have added too much flour.

If you're not using the dough straightaway, cover it with plastic wrap and set it aside for half an hour to rest (this is a great time to make your pasta sauce).

When you're ready to roll and cook the pasta, cut the dough ball in half. Dust some flour on your work surface and over a rolling pin or any other sturdy cylindrical object such as a wine bottle (which ideally should be readily available). Roll out one of the halves, keeping the other covered in plastic wrap, until it is flat enough to go through the pasta machine.

To roll the pasta, set the machine to its widest setting. Dust the dough with flour and carefully turn it through the machine, feeding it through the top and gently pulling it at the bottom. Remove the sheet of pasta, dust with flour, and fold the sheet over onto itself. This helps stretch out the dough and activates the gluten, which makes the pasta taste better.

Repeat this step twice more—after the third run, DO NOT FOLD the dough sheet. Turn the machine to the second-widest setting. From this point, put the pasta through each machine setting twice before moving on to the next. Always dust the pasta with flour after it goes through the machine (this is to prevent the pasta from sticking together once it is cut). You may need to cut the sheet in half as it can get quite long and tricky to handle. Repeat these steps until you have completed the thinnest setting on the pasta machine.

You can now turn the dough sheet into spaghetti, ravioli, pappardelle, et cetera. The type of pasta just depends on how you want to cut it. Remember to keep any dough or dough sheets you're not using covered so they don't dry out.

For spaghetti, run the dough sheet through the pasta machine on the spaghetti setting. Dust the cut pasta with flour and run it through the strands with your hands so that they do not stick together.

For ravioli, cut the dough sheet into squares and add 1 teaspoon of a filling of your choice. Brush the edges with water and top with a second pasta square, pressing down around the edges to seal them.

To cook fresh pasta, bring a large pot of water to a boil. Add the pasta and cook for at least 30 seconds but no longer than 60 seconds. It is scary how quickly fresh pasta cooks.

Drain and serve immediately with the sauce of your choice.

HOW TO IMPRESS A GIRL

Oh, boys, if only you knew how much cooking can swing the power back our way. Whether they will admit it or not, girls love it when a guy has made the effort to cook for them. How often have you asked your Ms. if she was free one night for dinner? I am sure that could very well be a common question; however, more than 95 percent of the time, guys are referring to dinner at a restaurant. When a woman comes home to find her man behind a skillet, creating something that smells amazing, the rest can only be imagined. Research suggests that these gestures cause the release of particular hormones—such as serotonin—which allow your woman to feel relaxed but also turned on. Whether you go the whole nine yards and set up a candlelit dinner or not, as long as you put on an apron, you are sure to get at least some sort of brownie points.

PERI-PERI ROAST CHICKEN

Serves 4

INGREDIENTS

The Stuffing . . .

1 cup couscous

1 teaspoon coriander seeds

1 teaspoon fennel seeds

2 teaspoons dried thyme, or 3 sprigs fresh thyme, chopped

Juice of 1/2 lemon, squeezed, flesh reserved

1 tablespoon extra-virgin olive oil

1/2 cup warm water

The Chicken . . .

1 (3 to 4 1/2-pound) whole chicken

4 tablespoons macadamia or extra-virgin olive oil

1 large sweet potato, peeled and cut into 3/8-inch-thick circles

3 zucchini, trimmed, halved crosswise, and cut lengthwise into 3/8-inch-thick pieces

3 Spanish onions, quartered

5 garlic cloves, crushed and finely chopped, plus 4 whole peeled garlic cloves

1 teaspoon salt

1 teaspoon black pepper

2 teaspoons smoked paprika

2 teaspoons red pepper flakes

Preheat the oven to 375°C.

To make the stuffing, place the couscous in a large bowl. Use a mortar and pestle to crush the coriander and fennel seeds into a fine powder and add them to the bowl with the couscous. Add the thyme, lemon juice, olive oil, and warm water and mix well. To stuff the chicken, hold the bird so that the cavity is facing upward, which makes it easier to spoon the mixture in. Fill the bird with the couscous. Use your hands to squash the stuffing down. Plug the end with the reserved juiced lemon half.

Pour 2 tablespoons of the oil over a roasting pan and set the chicken in the center of the pan. Surround it with the sweet potato, zucchini, and onions. Place the whole garlic cloves around the vegetables and sprinkle with a pinch of salt and pepper. Using a knife, cut three slashes into the chicken legs, as this will allow them to cook at the same time as the breast.

In a bowl, mix the chopped garlic, paprika, red pepper flakes, and the remaining salt, pepper, and 2 tablespoons of oil. Pour the mixture over the chicken and use your hands to coat the entire surface. You can also use a brush, but I find hands are much easier—just wash them well when you're done.

Roast the chicken for 1 1/4 hours. To check if it is ready, cut in between the leg and the breast. If the juices that run out are clear, the chicken is ready to be devoured. Spoon the couscous stuffing from the cavity into a dish and serve it alongside the chicken.

TIP: If you don't have a steamer, use a small metal colander.

POACHED SALMON WITH A WALNUT APPLE SALAD AND HONEY MUSTARD Serves 4

INGREDIENTS

The Salmon . . .

2 salmon fillets (around 7 ounces)

1 cup fish stock

2 lemongrass stalks, bashed with the side of your knife to release flavor

2 teaspoons fennel seeds

1 fennel bulb, trimmed and sliced

The Salad . . .

1 cucumber, cut lengthwise in ribbons with a vegetable peeler

1/2 cup walnuts

1 green apple, cored, halved, and thinly sliced

1 tablespoon parsley, finely chopped

The Honey Mustard Dressing . . .

1 tablespoon whole grain mustard

Juice of half a lemon

1 tablespoon honey

1/3 cup grapeseed/olive oil

Line a steamer with parchment paper and cut holes to allow steam through. Put the salmon on top of the baking paper and set aside.

In a saucepan, add the fish stock, fennel seeds, and lemongrass. Bring to a boil then turn the heat to low. Place the lined steamer on top and cover with a lid. Cook for 8 to 10 minutes. The salmon is ready when you can easily flake the fillet apart with a fork, revealing a wicked pink center.

Meanwhile, combine cucumber ribbons, toasted walnuts, apple, and parsley in a bowl.

If you have a glass jar, add the honey mustard ingredients and shake to combine. If you don't, mix ingredients together in a bowl.

Combine half the dressing with the salad mix and toss. Transfer to a serving dish.

Remove the salmon from the steamer. Allow the fish to rest for 3 minutes. With a fork, carefully peel the skin away from the fillets. Place the salmon on top of the salad. If the remaining dressing has been sitting for a while, give it another shake or stir before drizzling over the top to serve.

SWEET POTATO & LIME MASH
Serves 4

INGREDIENTS

2 large sweet potatoes, peeled and roughly chopped
Salt and black pepper
2 tablespoons extra-virgin olive oil

1 tablespoon grated fresh ginger
Zest and juice of 1 lime

Put the potatoes in a large saucepan with enough water to cover. Add a pinch of salt and bring to a boil over high heat. Cook until the potatoes are soft, about 8 minutes after the water has begun to boil. To check if they are soft, stick a skewer through the middle of a bigger piece. If it is stiff, keep cooking until the skewer goes through easily. Drain the potatoes into a colander (a metal or plastic bowl that has holes in it to drain liquid) and return them to the saucepan.

Here is the fun part—add the oil and use a masher (a fork will also work) to crush the potatoes so that there are no more solid bits remaining. If it has been a particularly hard day, this is a great way to let off a bit of steam. Get your shoulder involved, which will prevent your arms from fatiguing, as you end up using a bigger muscle group. To get it to a purée stage, use a hand mixer (the ends must be metal and not plastic, as they could melt).

Stir in the ginger, lime zest, and lime juice and season with salt and pepper to your liking.

INGREDIENTS

1/4 cup plain Greek yogurt

Handful of fresh mint, finely chopped

2 teaspoons chopped fresh chives

Zest of 1/2 lemon

Juice of 1 lemon

1 teaspoon grated fresh ginger

4 (7-ounce) whole trout or snapper, gutted and scaled (you can always get your fishmonger to do the dirty work for you)

2 scallions, white part only, thinly sliced

Salt and black pepper

Preheat the oven to 375°F. Set a baking sheet inside.

In a bowl, combine the yogurt, mint, chives, lemon zest, lemon juice, and ginger. Mix until well combined.

To create the bag, tear off four 8 by 12-inch sheets of parchment paper. Fold each sheet in half lengthwise, with the two long sides together, then twist the short ends tightly so that they don't unravel, to close the sides.

Place one fish in each bag and carefully spoon the yogurt mixture over each. Sprinkle with the scallions and some salt and pepper. Close the bag by curling the open side and finish by twisting the two corners.

Carefully remove the hot baking sheet from the oven and place the bags on it. They should sizzle from the heat. Bake for 8 to 10 minutes.

Serve the bags unopened, directly from the oven, on a plate with steamed rice or a fresh salad. The bags should be opened at the table—just be careful of the steam.

COCONUT MILK COCOA
Serves 2

INGREDIENTS

1 cup coconut milk

1 cup almond or dairy milk

1/2 cup cocoa nibs

1 teaspoon vanilla extract

1 tablespoon maple syrup

1 teaspoon ground cinnamon, or 1 (1-inch) cinnamon
   stick

1 teaspoon freshly grated nutmeg

Combine both milks in a saucepan. Cover and bring to a boil over high heat, then remove from the heat.

Add the cocoa nibs, vanilla, maple syrup, cinnamon, and nutmeg and cover. Let stand, stirring occasionally, for 10 minutes to infuse.

If you want a smoother texture, strain the mixture through a sieve into a mug. If not, ladle the cocoa directly into a mug.

TIP: Once you take them out of the oven, you must serve immediately as the soufflé will begin to fall. They should have a gooey center and be served hot.

CHOCOLATE SOUFFLÉ

Makes 4

INGREDIENTS

1 1/2 tablespoons unsalted butter, plus extra for the ramekins

2 teaspoons confectioners' sugar, plus extra for decorating

6 ounces dark chocolate, roughly chopped

2 tablespoons milk

4 egg whites

1/4 cup superfine sugar

3 egg yolks

1/2 teaspoon vanilla extract

Preheat the oven to 375°F. Butter the insides of 4 ramekins (small round ovenproof dishes) and dust each with ½ teaspoon of icing sugar. Rotate the ramekins so the sugar evenly coats them.

Bring an inch or two of water to a boil in a saucepan. Set a heatproof bowl over the saucepan, making sure the bottom does not touch the water. Place the butter and the chocolate in the bowl to melt, stirring occasionally to incorporate. As the chocolate begins to melt, add the milk and continue to stir. Keep a careful eye on the mixture—you don't want to overcook it. As soon as it becomes smooth, take it off the heat. Let cool for 5 minutes.

Meanwhile, in a large bowl, whisk the egg whites with a hand mixer until soft peaks form (when you pull the whisk out, the mixture should fold over on itself, not stand up straight). While whisking, gradually add the superfine sugar in three parts, making sure each addition has been incorporated before adding the next. Whisk until the egg whites are glossy and stiff peaks form (when you pull the whisk out, the mixture should be left standing tall like the peaks on a mountain).

Back to the chocolate sauce: Using a metal spoon, add one egg yolk at a time and stir until completely mixed in before adding the next. Stir in the vanilla extract.

Here is the tricky bit: The egg white mixture is full of air, and the more you mix it, the more air is lost. Air is important for the soufflé to rise in the oven. Pour the chocolate sauce into the egg whites, and using a flat spatula, fold the mixture gently from the outside in. Do not stir through the center. Continue to gently fold until completely mixed. Then, spoon the mixture evenly among the prepared ramekins. Remember, the mixture will rise, so do not fill the dishes up all the way. Set the ramekins on a baking sheet, carefully transfer to the oven, and bake for 8 minutes.

Immediately dust the soufflés with confectioners' sugar, and serve hot.

RHUBARB & VANILLA CREAM

Makes 4

INGREDIENTS

1 bunch rhubarb stems, chopped

1 tablespoon brown sugar

1/4 cup old-fashioned rolled oats

1 teaspoon ground cinnamon

3 graham crackers or arrowroot biscuits (whatever you choose should be slightly sweet)

2 tablespoons flaxseed oil (optional)

1/2 handful of macadamia nuts

1 cup heavy cream (for a healthier version, use plain yogurt and replace the sugar with a teaspoon of honey)

1 teaspoon superfine sugar

1 teaspoon vanilla extract

In a saucepan, combine the rhubarb, brown sugar, and 1 tablespoon water, cover, and cook over low heat, stirring regularly, for 6 to 8 minutes. The rhubarb is done when it has reduced to resemble a thick sauce, almost like a stew; however, some of the chunks should still hold their shape.

Meanwhile, combine the oats, cinnamon, graham crackers, flaxseed oil (if using), and macadamias in a blender and pulse until coarse. (If you don't have a blender, place the graham crackers and macadamias in a folded tea towel and lightly bash them with a rolling pin. Then transfer them to a bowl and stir in the oats, cinnamon, and flaxseed oil until it looks like a very coarse crumble.) Transfer the crumbs to a dry skillet and toast them for 1 minute over low heat.

In a bowl, whisk together the cream, superfine sugar, and vanilla with a hand mixer until the cream no longer falls off a spoon when turned upside down. If you skipped the gym, test your arms and use a whisk, but make sure to avoid spillage when you crank up the pace. Set aside until ready to serve.

To serve, dish the rhubarb equally among four glasses and place a dollop of cream on top (if you can, use a piping bag to avoid touching the sides for amazing presentation; if you don't have a piping bag, a Ziploc bag with a corner cut out works as well). Finish with a sprinkling of the biscuit crumbs over the top.

INGREDIENTS

The Shortbread . . .	The Ganache . . .
12 tablespoons (1 1/2 sticks) unsalted butter, plus extra for the pan	Handful of hazelnuts or macadamia nuts (optional)
1/2 teaspoon salt	1 teaspoon ground cinnamon
1 cup all-purpose flour	Handful of walnuts
1/4 cup sugar	1 (7-ounce) block dark chocolate, roughly broken
	6 tablespoons heavy cream
	1/2 pint raspberries
	1 teaspoon vanilla extract

To make the shortbread base, preheat the oven to 350°F. Butter a springform pan.

Cut the butter into 1/2-inch cubes and place them in the bowl of a food processor. Add the remaining shortbread ingredients and process until the mixture forms small lumps. Press the shortbread mixture into the prepared pan, using the back of a spoon to flatten the mixture down. (You could also use a rimmed baking sheet—just make sure it isn't too big or the base will be too thin.) Bake until the shortbread is golden, about 20 minutes. Let cool in the pan.

To make the ganache, place the nuts in a plastic bag and then put that bag inside another; seal both bags. Using a rolling pin, carefully crush the nuts into smaller chunks. You don't want them too fine. (This step can also be done in a food processor.)

Bring an inch or two of water to a boil in a saucepan. Set a heatproof bowl over the saucepan, making sure the bottom does not touch the water. Place the chocolate in the bowl to melt, stirring occasionally. Gradually add the cream, adding a bit and stirring it in to completely incorporate before adding more. At this stage, the chocolate will thicken up. Take it off the heat. Stir in the raspberries; their juice will make the mixture runnier. Stir in the crushed nuts and the vanilla.

Pour the ganache over the shortbread base and spread it into an even layer with the back of a spoon. Cover and refrigerate for 30 minutes. Remove the outer ring of the springform pan and using the edge of a knife, carefully loosen the bottom of the shortbread before sliding it onto a plate or cutting board to be sliced and shared.

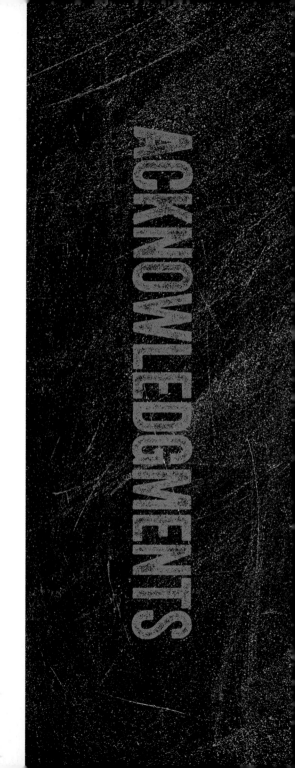

The Boys

Thanks for putting your hands up and taking the time to eat all of the food. Not to mention getting your photo taken. Tough gig.

Churchill Family

My cooking began in Mum and Dad's house. If we all have something in common, it would be a love of food. Mum and Dad, I thank you for bringing us boys up the way you have. We would not be who we are today without you. Judging and critiquing each other's meals has developed my knowledge of flavors. I hope you understand how much of an influence all four of you are on my life.

W. Lance Reynolds

I can't put into words my gratitude for meeting you. I never thought I would find anyone who would work as hard for my vision. Thank you. We have so much to do, but I have all the faith in the world.

Simon & Schuster

I made this book on the floor of my bedroom, and it is now global. For the belief in a vision and understanding my passion—thank you. There is no doubt you will be a part of my life for many years to come.

Emily Graff

One truly epic editor. You have put up with my antics. You are professional, you seriously love food, and you have a drive for success that is inspiring. I can't wait to work with you for many, many, many years. You are not going anywhere.

INDEX

A

apples: Poached Salmon with Walnut Apple Salad and Honey Mustard, 112, 113

arugula: (Friggin') Amazing Salad, 50, 51

asparagus:

Chicken Curry, 20, 21

Chicken Stir-Fry with Brown Basmati Rice, 62, 63

avocado:

Chicken Avo Pie, 18, 19

Herbed Chicken Wrap, 34, 35

Pizza in a Pan, 48, 49

B

balls:

Chicken & Herb Balls with Garlic Aioli, 78, 79

Lamb Meatball Wrap, 82, 83

bananas: Choc-Banana Protein Shake, 32, 33

Basic Bro Burger, 54, 55

basil:

Harissa Chicken Drummies with Cooling Basil Yogurt, 80, 81

Pesto, 92, 93

beans:

Bison Hoisin & Greens, 64, 65

Chicken Avo Pie, 18, 19

Chicken Curry, 20, 21

Chicken Stir-Fry with Brown Basmati Rice, 62, 63

Hummus with Honey Parsnip Chips, 96, 97

Oven Breakfast Dip, 76, 77

bean sprouts:

Chicken Curry, 20, 21

San Choy Bow, 66, 67

beef:

Basic Bro Burger, 54, 55

Marinated Sirloin with Pea Mash, 38, 39

San Choy Bow, 66, 67

Slow-Roasted Beef, 22, 23

Spag Bol (Spaghetti Bolognese), 26, 27

Summer Beef Roast, 36, 37

berries:

Berry Compote French Toast with Caramel
Sauce, 44, 45

Brekkie on the Go, 46, 47

Fruit Soup, 70, 71

Getting Out of the Doghouse, 124, 125

Oven-Baked Peach Surprise, 72, 73

Bison Hoisin & Greens, 64, 65

blender or food processor, 14

bok choi:

Bison Hoisin & Greens, 64, 65

Chicken Curry, 20, 21

breads:

Berry Compote French Toast with Caramel
Sauce, 44, 45

Olive Oil Pita Chips, 98, 99

Toad in a Hole, 50, 51

Brekkie on the Go, 46, 47

broccoli:

Chicken Stir-Fry with Brown Basmati Rice,
62, 63

broccolini:

Bison Hoisin & Greens, 64, 65

brownies:

Protein Brownies, 40, 41

C

cacao, see chocolate

Caramel Sauce, 44, 45

carbohydrates, 57–58

cheese:

(Friggin') Amazing Salad, 50, 51

Basic Bro Burger, 54, 55

Chicken & Herb Balls with Garlic Aioli, 78,
79

Chicken Avo Pie, 18, 19

Inside-Out Spicy Omelet, 52, 53

Pesto, 92, 93

Pizza in a Pan, 48, 49

Spag Bol (Spaghetti Bolognese), 26, 27

Squash Blossoms, 102, 103

San Choy Bow, 66, 67

Sweet Potato Patties, 24

Sweet Potato Strips, 86, 87